This Land I Love

This Land I Love

Edited by Arthur Wortman

*Inspirational Writings
About the Real Meaning of America
By a Host of Famous People
From Patrick Henry to John Wayne*

♛ HALLMARK EDITIONS

Third verse of "O Beautiful, My Country" by Frederick Lucian Hosmer from *Hymns of the Spirit*. Copyright © 1937 by Beacon Press. Reprinted by permission of Beacon Press. "The Full-Fledged American" by Struthers Burt. Reprinted by permission of Mrs. Katherine Newlin Burt. "First Impressions of the U.S.A." taken from *Ideas and Opinions* by Albert Einstein. © 1954 by Crown Publishers, Inc. Used by permission of Crown Publishers, Inc. "I have a dream..." by Martin Luther King, Jr. Reprinted by permission of Joan Daves. Copyright © 1963 by Martin Luther King, Jr. "Freedom From Prejudice" from *Declaration of Conscience* by Margaret Chase Smith. Copyright © 1972 by Margaret Chase Smith. Reprinted by permission of Doubleday & Company, Inc. "A Land of Dedication and Dreams" from "Believing in America Is Making It Work" by Rose Kennedy from *Ladies' Home Journal* (January, 1974). © 1973 Downe Publishing, Inc. Reprinted by permission of *Ladies' Home Journal* and Mrs. Joseph P. Kennedy. "Principles on Which This Nation Is Based" from pp. xvi-xvii in *Tomorrow Is Now* by Eleanor Roosevelt. Copyright © 1963 by the Estate of Anna Eleanor Roosevelt. Reprinted by permission of Harper & Row, Publishers, Inc. and Nannine Joseph, agent for Estate of Anna Eleanor Roosevelt. Excerpt from *Inside U.S.A.* by John Gunther. Copyright 1947 by John Gunther. Reprinted by permission of Harper & Row, Publishers, Inc., and Hamish Hamilton Ltd., Publishers. Excerpt from *Dodsworth* by Sinclair Lewis. Reprinted by permission of Harcourt Brace Jovanovich, Inc., and Jonathan Cape Limited. "A Nation That Looks Forward" from *The Wave of the Future* by Anne Morrow Lindbergh. Reprinted by permission of Harcourt Brace Jovanovich, Inc. "Rugged Individualism" from *The Challenge to Liberty* by Herbert Hoover. Used by permission of The Herbert Hoover Foundation. "The Gift Outright" from *The Poetry of Robert Frost* edited by Edward Connery Lathem. Copyright 1942 by Robert Frost. Copyright © 1969 by Holt, Rinehart and Winston, Inc. Copyright © 1970 by Lesley Frost Ballantine. Reprinted by permission of Holt, Rinehart and Winston, Inc., the Estate of Robert Frost and Jonathan Cape Ltd. "The American Animal" from *Autobiography of Will Rogers*, edited by Donald Day. Published by Houghton Mifflin Company. Copyright © 1949 by The Rogers Company. Used by permission of Houghton Mifflin Company and Donald Day. "The Meaning of 'Moving West'" by Archibald MacLeish. First appeared in *Collier's*, July 8, 1955. Reprinted by permission of the American. "Living Testimony to the American Dream" from "The American Dream" by Eric Sevareid from *Look*, July 8, 1968. Copyright by Eric Sevareid, 1968. Reprinted by permission of The Harold Matson Company, Inc. Excerpt from *What America Means to Me* by Pearl S. Buck reprinted by permission of Harold Ober Associates Incorporated. Copyright 1942, 1943 by Pearl S. Buck. Copyright renewed. "Freedom of Choice" from the book *'Twixt Twelve and Twenty* by Pat Boone. © 1958 by Prentice-Hall, Inc. Published by Prentice-Hall, Inc., Englewood Cliffs, New Jersey. Reprinted by permission. "'Palace' of the World" from the book *The Way I See It* by Eddie Cantor. © 1959 by Eddie Cantor. Published by Prentice-Hall, Inc., Englewood Cliffs, New Jersey. Reprinted by permission. "An Inner Air, An Inner Light" from *Major Campaign Speeches of Adlai E. Stevenson, 1952* by Adlai E. Stevenson. Copyright 1953 by Random House, Inc. Reprinted by permission of Random House, Inc. "They Called It America" by Rabbi Abba Hillel Silver from *Sunshine Magazine* (July, 1966). Reprinted with permission of *Sunshine Magazine*. "The American Flag: 'It's Just a Piece of Cloth'" from *Sunshine Magazine* (June, 1965). Reprinted with permission of *Sunshine Magazine*. "Our Continuing Revolution" from *America and Americans* by John Steinbeck. Copyright © 1966 by John Steinbeck. All Rights Reserved. Reprinted by permission of The Viking Press, Inc. "A New Twist on Opportunity" from *The Washington Wits*, edited by Bill Adler, 1967, published by The Macmillan Company. Copyright © 1967 by Bill Adler. Reprinted by permission of Bill Adler. "The Foundation in Religious Freedom" by Sam Ervin, Jr., from *The Wisdom of Sam Ervin*, edited by Bill M. Wise. © 1973 by Bill M. Wise. Reprinted by permission. "America Is an Attitude" from an address by John Wayne to the Republican National Convention in Miami Beach on August 5, 1968. Reprinted by permission of John Wayne.

Design: Eva Sue Szela and Rick Cusick. Production Art: Judi Howen.

Copyright © 1975 by Hallmark Cards, Inc., Kansas City, Missouri. All Rights Reserved. Printed in the United States of America. Library of Congress Catalog Card Number: 74-76161. Standard Book Number: 87529-390-5.

This Land I Love

Walt Whitman
I Hear America Singing

I hear America singing, the varied carols I hear,
Those of mechanics, each one singing his as it
　should be blithe and strong,
The carpenter singing his as he measures his plank
　or beam,
The mason singing his as he makes ready for work,
　or leaves off work,
The boatman singing what belongs to him in his boat,
　the deckhand singing on the steamboat deck,
The shoemaker singing as he sits on his bench, the
　hatter singing as he stands,
The wood-cutter's song, the ploughboy's on his way
　in the morning, or at the noon intermission
　or at sun-down;
The delicious singing of the mother, or of the
　young wife at work, or of the girl
　sewing or washing,
Each singing what belongs to her, and to none else;
The day what belongs to the day — at night,
　the party of young fellows, robust, friendly,
Singing with open mouths their strong melodious
　songs.

Sinclair Lewis

Intellectually I know that America is no better than any other country; emotionally I know she is better than every other country.

Henry Kissinger
...A Personal Meaning
of America's Greatness

On September 22, 1973, Henry Kissinger, once an immigrant from Germany, was sworn in as Secretary of State. Thus he became the first naturalized citizen in American history to hold this high office. In introducing Kissinger to the assembled guests, President Nixon spoke of this distinction, and Kissinger in turn made this reply.

Mr. President, you referred to my background, and it is true, there is no country in the world where it is conceivable that a man of my origin could be standing here next to the President of the United States. And if my origin can contribute anything to the formulation of our policy, it is that at an early age I have seen what can happen to a society that is based on hatred and strength and distrust, and that I experienced then what America means to other people, its hope and its idealism. And therefore, in achieving a structure of peace under your leadership, Mr. President, we will strive not just for a pragmatic solution to this or that difficulty, but to recognize that America has never been true to itself unless it meant something beyond itself.

And as we work for a world at peace with justice, compassion, and humanity, we know that America, in fulfilling man's deepest aspirations, fulfills what is best within it.

Sam Ervin, Jr.
...*The Foundation in Religious Freedom*

The men and women who gave liberty to America were devout souls. They had learned some of the sorrowful facts of the spiritual life of man in the bitter crucible of experience. Most of them dissented from the doctrines and usages of the churches established by laws in the lands of their origins. They were denied the right to worship God in their own ways. They were compelled to pay tithes for the support and propagation of religious opinions which they disbelieved. They had their marriages annulled and their children adjudged illegitimate for daring to speak their marriage vows before ministers of their own faiths rather than before clergymen of the established churches.

But these cruel oppressions merely steeled their convictions that religion is a private matter between man and his God; that no human authority should undertake to control or interfere with the rights of conscience; and that "to compel a man to furnish contributions of money for the propagation of opinions which he disbelieves is sinful and tyrannical."

For these reasons, our ancestors staked the very existence of America as a free nation upon the principle that all men have a natural and unalienable right to worship Almighty God according to the dictates of their own consciences, and the corollary that this natural and unalienable right can be secured only by keeping the hands of the state out of religion and the hands of religion off the state.

George Washington
...From His *"Farewell Address"*

...CITIZENS, by birth or choice, of a common country, that country has a right to concentrate your affections. The name of AMERICAN, which belongs to you in your national capacity, must always exalt the just pride of patriotism more than any appellation derived from local discriminations. With slight shades of difference you have the same religion, manners, habits, and political principles. You have in a common cause fought and triumphed together; the independence and liberty you possess are the work of joint councils and joint efforts, of common dangers, sufferings, and successes....

Observe good faith and justice toward all nations; cultivate peace and harmony with all. Religion and morality enjoin this conduct, and can it be that good policy does not equally enjoin it? It will be worthy of a free, enlightened, and, at no distant period, a great nation, to give to mankind the magnanimous and too novel example of a people always guided by an exalted justice and benevolence. Who can doubt that, in the course of time and things, the fruits of such a plan would richly repay any temporary advantages which might be lost by a steady adherence to it? Can it be that Providence has not connected the permanent felicity of a nation with its virtue? The experiment, at least, is recommended by every sentiment which ennobles human nature.

I believe in America...

John Steinbeck
...Our Continuing Revolution

Something happened in America to create the Americans. Perhaps it was the grandeur of the land—the lordly mountains, the mystery of deserts, the ache of storms, cyclones—the enormous sweetness and violence of the country which, acting on restless, driven peoples from the outside world, made them taller than their ancestors, stronger than their fathers—and made them all Americans....

From the beginning, in hindsight at least, our social direction is clear. We have moved to become one people out of many.... We have failed sometimes, taken wrong paths, paused for renewal, filled our bellies and licked our wounds, but we have never slipped back—never.

Margaret Chase Smith
...Freedom From Prejudice

If there be any doubter of the relative freedom of Americans from bigotry and hatred as compared to the other peoples of the world, then let him take a good long look at the Statue of Liberty and particularly those words inscribed at its base:

"Give me your tired, your poor,
your huddled masses yearning to breathe free,
the wretched refuse of your teeming shore.
Send these, the homeless,
tempest-tossed, to me...."

Pat Boone
...Freedom of Choice

...How many times have you put your hand over your heart, looked at the Stars and Stripes, and said: "I pledge allegiance to the flag of the United States of America and to the republic for which it stands, one nation under God, indivisible, with liberty and justice for all."? I know. I can't count 'em either. But an important part of my growing up was to begin to realize what this meant.

It means that every single one of us is free to choose, "under God," what we wish to do with our lives. It means we, you, me, your Aunt Minnie, the boy across the street, we are all free to live where we choose, say what we choose, write what we choose, worship as we choose, work as we choose, and we also have the all-American right to gripe. We can dream the biggest dream we can conceive and it can come true.

John Gunther

Ours is the only country deliberately founded on a good idea.

Woodrow Wilson

Sometimes people call me an idealist. Well, that is the way I know I am an American. America is the only idealistic country in the world.

...an inner light in which freedom lives...

Albert Einstein
...First Impressions of the U.S.A.

I must...say something about my impressions of this country. That is not altogether easy for me. For it is not easy to take up the attitude of impartial observer when one is received with such kindness and undeserved respect as I have been in America....

What first strikes the visitor with amazement is the superiority of this country in matters of technology and organization. Objects of everyday use are more solid than in Europe, houses much more practically designed. Everything is designed to save human labor....

The second thing that strikes a visitor is the joyous, positive attitude to life. The smile on the faces of the people in photographs is symbolical of one of the greatest assets of the American. He is friendly, self-confident, optimistic — and without envy.

Martin Luther King, Jr.
"I have a dream..."

I say to you today, my friends, that in spite of the difficulties and frustrations of the moment I still have a dream. It is a dream deeply rooted in the American dream.

I have a dream that one day this nation will rise up and live out the true meaning of its creed: "We hold these truths to be self-evident; that all men are created equal."

I have a dream that one day on the red hills of

Georgia the sons of former slaves and the sons of former slaveowners will be able to sit down together at the table of brotherhood....

This will be the day when all of God's children will be able to sing with a new meaning "My country 'tis of thee, sweet land of liberty, of thee I sing. Land where my fathers died, land of the pilgrim's pride, from every mountainside, let freedom ring."

And if America is to be a great nation this must become true. So let freedom ring from the prodigious hilltops of New Hampshire. Let freedom ring from the mighty mountains of New York. Let freedom ring from the heightening Alleghenies of Pennsylvania!

Let freedom ring from the snowcapped Rockies of Colorado!

Let freedom ring from the curvaceous peaks of California!

But not only that; let freedom ring from Stone Mountain in Georgia!

Let freedom ring from Lookout Mountain of Tennessee!

Let freedom ring from every hill and molehill of Mississippi. From every mountainside, let freedom ring.

When we let freedom ring, when we let it ring from every village and every hamlet, from every state and every city, we will be able to speed up that day when all of God's children, black men and white men, Jews and Gentiles, Protestants and Catholics, will be able to join hands and sing the words of the old Negro spiritual, "Free at last! free at last! thank God Almighty, we are free at last!"

The American Flag:
'It's Just a Piece of Cloth'

That is all it is — just a piece of cloth.

But when a little breeze comes along it stirs and comes to life, and flutters and snaps in the wind, all red and white and blue! And then you realize that no other piece of cloth could be like it!

It has your whole life wrapped up in it — the meals you eat; the time you spend with your family; the kind of things your boy and girl learn at school; the strange and wonderful thoughts you get in church on Sunday.

Those stars in it — they make you feel just as free as the stars in the wide, deep night. And those stripes — they are bars of blood to any dictator who would try to change this way of life.

Just a piece of cloth, that is all — until you put your soul into it, and give it a meaning. Then it is a symbol of liberty, and decency, and fair-dealing for everyone. It is just a piece of cloth until we breathe life into it; until we make it stand for everything we believe in, and refuse to live without it.

From SUNSHINE MAGAZINE

Pearl Buck

We Americans are like natural rock. Our glory and our strength are in our naturalness; in saying what we think, unashamed, in doing what we feel is right, unafraid.

Wendell Willkie
...One Man's Creed

I believe in America because in it we are free — free to choose our government, to speak our minds, to observe our different religions. Because we are generous with our freedom, we share our rights with those who disagree with us. Because we hate no people and covet no people's lands. Because we are blessed with a natural and varied abundance. Because we have great dreams and because we have the opportunity to make those dreams come true.

Struthers Burt
...The Full-Fledged American

Were I to have a vision of a full-fledged American it would be something like this: A man who, with sufficient knowledge of the past, would walk fairly constantly with the thought that he was blood-brother, if not by actual race then by the equally subtle method of mental vein transfusing into mental vein, of Washington and Lincoln; of Jefferson and Lee, and of all the men like them. Who would walk, because of this, carefully and proudly, and also humbly, lest he fail them. And, with a keen sense of the present and the future, would say to himself: "I am an American and therefore what I do, however small, is of importance."

Jane Addams
...Of Patriotism and Great Men

As a pioneering social worker in the poor neighborhoods of Chicago, Jane Addams ultimately touched the conscience of the world and received the Nobel Peace Prize. On Washington's Birthday in 1903, she delivered a moving address on patriotism and America's great men.

We meet together upon these birthdays of our great men, not only to review their lives, but to revive and cherish our own patriotism. This matter is a difficult task. In the first place, we are prone to think that by merely reciting these great deeds we get a reflected glory, and that the future is secure to us because the past has been so fine.

In the second place, we are apt to think that we inherit the fine qualities of those great men simply because we have had a common descent and are living in the same territory....

What is a great man who has made his mark upon history? Every time, if we think far enough, he is a man who has looked through the confusion of the moment and has seen the moral issue involved; he is a man who has refused to have his sense of justice distorted; he has listened to his conscience until conscience becomes a trumpet call to like-minded men, so that they gather about him and together, with mutual purpose and mutual aid, they make a new period in history....

A wise patriotism, which will take hold of...questions by careful legal enactment, by constant and vigorous enforcement, because of the belief that if the meanest man in the Republic is deprived of his rights, then every man in the Republic is deprived of his rights, is the only patriotism by which public-spirited men and women, with a thoroughly aroused conscience, can worthily serve this Republic. Let us say again that the lessons of great men are lost unless they re-enforce upon our minds the highest demands which we make upon ourselves; that they are lost unless they drive our sluggish wills forward in the direction of their highest ideals.

Patrick Henry
...Give Me Liberty or Give Me Death

Patrick Henry's speech in the Virginia Convention, March 23, 1775, was considered close to treason by some... perhaps because it so vehemently summed up the spirit to become an independent nation.

It is in vain, sir, to extenuate the matter. Gentlemen may cry, "Peace! peace!" — but there is no peace. The war is actually begun! The next gale that sweeps from the north will bring to our ears the clash of resounding arms! Our brethren are already in the field! Why stand we here idle? What is it that gentlemen wish? What would they have? Is life so dear, or peace so sweet, as to be purchased at the price of chains and slavery? Forbid it, Almighty God! I know not what course others may take; but as for me, give me liberty or give me death!

Samuel Francis Smith
America

My country, 'tis of thee,
Sweet land of liberty,
   Of thee I sing;
Land where my fathers died,
Land of the pilgrims' pride,
From every mountain-side
   Let Freedom ring.

My native country, thee,
Land of the noble free, —
   Thy name I love;
I love thy rocks and rills,
Thy woods and templed hills;
My heart with rapture thrills
   Like that above.

Let music swell the breeze,
And ring from all the trees
   Sweet Freedom's song;
Let mortal tongues awake,
Let all that breathe partake,
Let rocks their silence break,
   The sound prolong.

Our fathers' God, to Thee,
Author of liberty,
   To Thee we sing;
Long may our land be bright
With Freedom's holy light;
Protect us by Thy might,
   Great God, our King.

Don Raye and Al Jacobs

From *"This Is My Country"*

This is my country!
   Land of my birth.
This is my country!
   Grandest on earth!
I pledge thee my allegiance.
   America the bold.
For this is my country,
   To have to hold!

From This Is My Country, music by Al Jacobs, words by Don Raye.
©Copyright MCMXL, Shawnee Press, Inc., Delaware Water Gap, Pa. 18327.
U.S. Copyright Renewed MCMLXVIII. Used by permission.

...the only idealistic country in the world.

Anne Morrow Lindbergh
...A Nation That Looks Forward

We have been a nation who looked forward to new ideals, not back to old legends. A nation who preferred pioneering new paths to following old ruts; a nation who pinned its faith on dreams rather than on memories. Surely, among all the nations of the world it could best be sung of us:

>"We are the music makers
>And we are the dreamers of dreams."

Alfred J. Beveridge

The twentieth century will be American. American thought will dominate it. American progress will give it color and direction. American deeds will make it illustrious.

Eddie Cantor
...The 'Palace' of the World

All my life, America's been called a "melting pot." I say it's not — and I hope it won't become one. A melting pot has just one purpose. To dissolve all differences. To make all things alike. That's not America. I'd rather think of us in terms of the theater. The Palace of the world. Where any act is welcome if it helps the show in toto. Where variety is recognized — not as the spice of life, but life itself.

The Honorable Carl Albert
...A New Twist on Opportunity

America is indeed the land of opportunity, but sometimes that idea takes a surprising turn, as Speaker of the House Carl Albert relates in one of his favorite stories.

I am quite short in physical stature, only five feet four inches tall. I was speaking at a rural school in my district and was giving the audience everything I had. At the conclusion of my speech, a little boy came up to me and said, "Mister, you sure inspired me today."

I beamed at the lad and pursued the matter a little further. I asked him what I had said that had been inspiring, thinking that whatever it was, I could use it on another audience.

"It wasn't anything you said," replied the boy. "I just figure if a little squirt like you can be elected to Congress, I can become President of the United States."

John F. Kennedy
...The Arts in America

I see little of more importance to the future of our country or civilization than full recognition of the place of the artist. If art is to nourish the roots of our culture, society must set the artist free to follow his vision wherever it takes him....For art establishes the basic human truths which must serve as the touchstones of our judgment.

Will Rogers
...The American Animal (1925)

When an Office Holder, or one that has been found out, can't think of anything to deliver a speech on, he always falls back on the good old subject, Americanism. Now that is the only thing I have never delivered an Essay on, either written or spoken. They have all had a crack at it every Fourth of July and Lincoln's Birthday. So now I am going to take up the subject and see what I can wrestle out of it. Let's get our rope ready and turn it out, and we will catch it and see really what brands it has on it. Here it comes out of the Corral. We got it caught; now it's throwed and Hog Tied; and we will pick the Brands and see what they are.

The first thing I find out is there ain't any such animal. This American Animal that I thought I had here is nothing but the big Honest Majority, that you might find in any Country. He is not a Politician, he is a 100% American, he is not any organization, either uplift or down fall. In fact I find he don't belong to anything. He has no decided Political faith or religion. I can't even find out what religious brand is on him. From his earmarks he has never made a speech, and announced that he was An American. He hasn't denounced anything. It looks to me like he is just an Animal that has been going along, believing in right, doing right, tending to his own business, and letting the other fellows alone.

He don't seem to be simple enough minded to believe that EVERYTHING is right and he don't appear to be Cuckoo enough to think that EVERYTHING is wrong. He don't seem to be a Prodigy and he don't seem to be a Simp. In fact, all I can find out about him is that he is just NORMAL. After I let him up and get on my Horse and ride away I look around and see hundreds and hundreds of exactly the same marks and Brands. In fact they so far outnumber the freakly branded ones that the only conclusion I can come to is that this Normal breed is so far in the majority that there is no use to worry about the others. They are a lot of Mavericks and Strays.

The Inscription on Plymouth Rock Monument

This monument marks the first burying ground in Plymouth of the passengers of the Mayflower.

Here, under cover of darkness, the fast dwindling company laid their dead, leveling the earth above them lest the Indians should know how many were the graves. Reader! History records no nobler venture for faith and freedom than of this Pilgrim band. In weariness and painfulness, in watchings, often in hunger and cold, they laid the foundations of a state wherein every man, through countless ages, should have liberty to worship God in his own way. May their example inspire thee to do thy part in perpetuating and spreading the lofty ideas of our republic throughout the world!

Frederick L. Hosmer
From "O Beautiful, My Country"

O beautiful, our country!
   Round thee in love we draw;
Thine is the grace of freedom,
   The majesty of law.
Be righteousness thy scepter,
   Justice thy diadem;
And on thy shining forehead
   Be peace the crowning gem.

Lady Bird Johnson *(From speech on March 31, 1964)*

It is a good time to be a woman in America because your country, more now than at any time in its history, is utilizing your abilities and intelligence.

Herbert Hoover *…"Rugged Individualism"*
The Challenge to Liberty

While I can make no claim for having introduced the term "rugged individualism," I should be proud to have invented it. It has been used by American leaders for over a half-century in eulogy of those God-fearing men and women of honesty whose stamina and character and fearless assertion of rights led them to make their own way in life.

John Greenleaf Whittier   *Centennial Hymn*

(*Composed in 1876, on America's 100th anniversary*)

Our fathers' God! from out whose hand
The centuries fall like grains of sand,
We meet today, united, free,
And loyal to our land and Thee,
To thank Thee for the era done,
And trust Thee for the opening one.

For art and labor met in truce,
For beauty made the bride of use,
We thank Thee; but, withal, we crave
The austere virtues strong to save,
The honor proof to place or gold,
The manhood never bought or sold!

Oh, make Thou us, through centuries long,
In peace secure, in justice strong;
Around our gift of freedom draw
The safeguards of thy righteous law:
And, cast in some diviner mold,
Let the new cycle shame the old!

Henry W. Grady

Let it be understood in my parting words to you that I am no pessimist as to this republic. I always bet on sunshine in America.

Rabbi Abba Hillel Silver
...They Called It America

God built him a continent of glory, and filled it with treasures untold. He studded it with sweet-flowing fountains, and traced it with long-winding streams. He carpeted it with soft-rolling prairies, and columned it with thundering mountains. He graced it with deep-shadowed forests, and filled them with song.

Then He called unto a thousand peoples, and summoned the bravest among them. They came from the ends of the earth, each bearing a gift and a hope. The glow of adventure was in their eyes, and in their hearts the glory of hope.

And out of the bounty of earth, and the labor of men; out of the longing of heart, and the prayer of souls; out of the memory of ages, and the hopes of the world, God fashioned a nation in love, and blessed it with purpose sublime.

And they called it America.

Benjamin Harrison
...The Condition of Our Gifts

No other people have a government more worthy of their respect and love, or a land so magnificent in extent, so pleasant to look upon, and so full of generous suggestion to enterprise and labor....

Eric Sevareid

...Living Testimony
to the American Dream

One day recently, I asked a Cuban refugee why most Cubans like himself wanted to come to the United States rather than go to Latin American countries with the same language and the same general culture. Was it just the thought of greater economic opportunity?

"No," he said, "many of us would have an easier time, economically, in a Latin country. It's just that we feel better here. We can feel like a human being. There seems to be something universal about this country."

This is living testimony, not abstract argument, from men who know the meaning of America in their bones and marrow. Of course, it is the truth. Of course, the dream lives on.

Stephen Decatur

OUR COUNTRY! In her intercourse with foreign nations may she always be in the right; but our country, right or wrong.

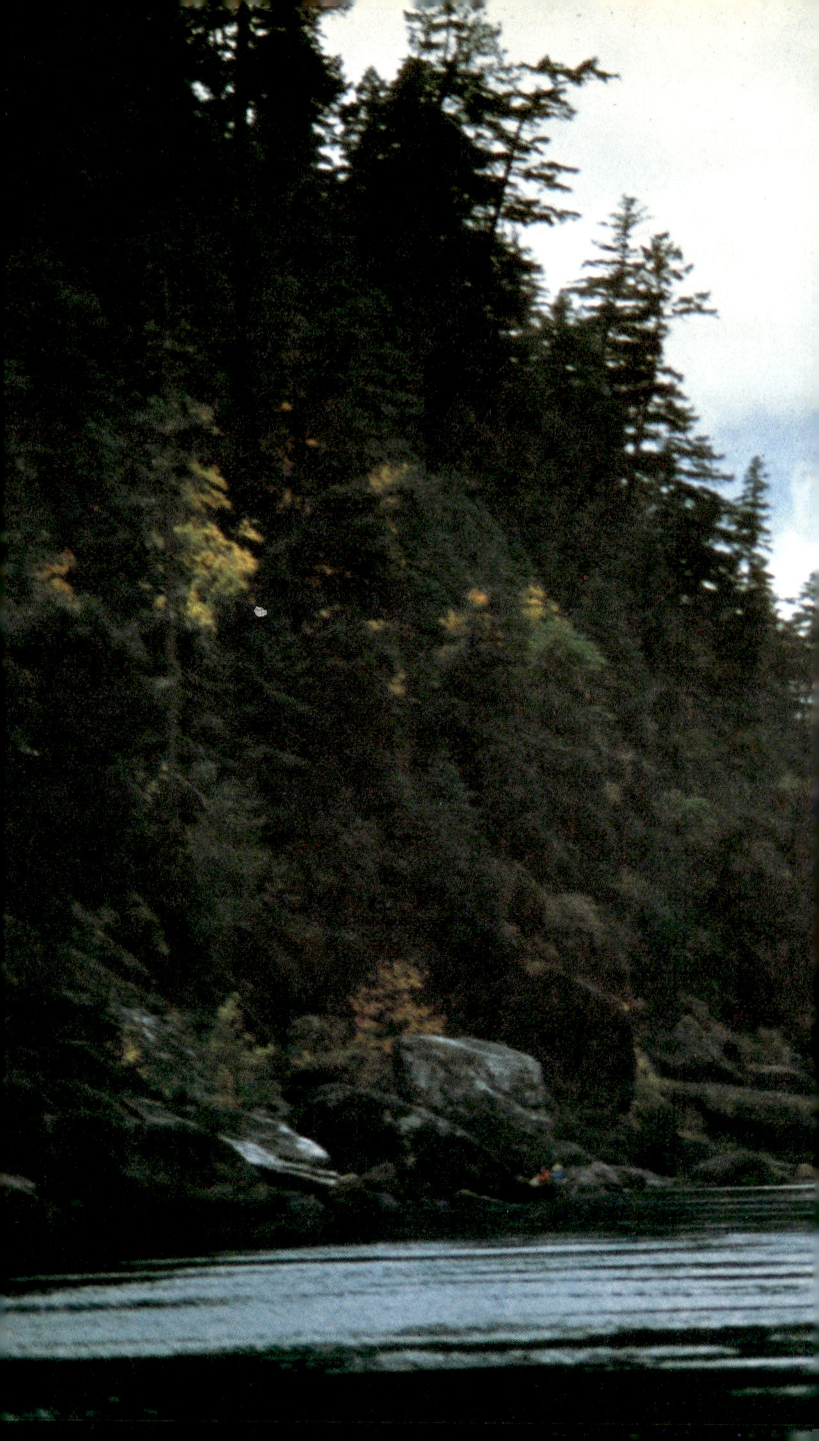

Sweet land of liberty...

Adlai Stevenson
...An Inner Air, An Inner Light

When an American says that he loves his country, he means not only that he loves the New England hills, the prairies glistening in the sun, the wide and rising plains, the great mountains, and the sea. He means that he loves an inner air, an inner light in which freedom lives and in which a man can draw the breath of self-respect.

Men who have offered their lives for their country know that patriotism is not the *fear* of something; it is the *love* of something. Patriotism with us is not the hatred of Russia; it is the love of this Republic and of the ideal of liberty of man and mind in which it was born, and to which this Republic is dedicated.

Eleanor Roosevelt
...Principles on Which This Nation Is Based

It is essential to turn back to our history now and then to remind ourselves of the principles on which this nation is based.... We could never have conquered the wilderness, never have built the foundations of a country and a new concept of life, based on the fullest and freest development of the individual; never have overcome vast difficulties and dangers, if we had not had a new idea, an idea so noble in concept that it gave us confidence in ourselves and gave us the strength to build this new nation, step by step.

John Wayne
...America Is an Attitude

I have a feeling that a nation is more than just government, laws and rules. It's an attitude. It's the people's outlook. Dean Martin once asked me what I wanted for my baby daughter, and I realize now that my answer was a kind of an attitude toward my country....

I told him that I wanted for my daughter, Marisa, what most parents want for their children. I wanted to stick around long enough to see that she got a good start, and I would like to have her know some of the values that we knew as kids, some of the values that an articulate few now are saying are old-fashioned. But most of all I want her to be grateful, as I am grateful for every day of my life that I spend in the United States of America....

I don't care whether she ever memorizes the Gettysburg Address or not, but I want her to understand it, and since very few little girls are asked to defend their country, she will probably never have to raise her hand to that oath, but I want her to respect all who do.

Thomas Jefferson   ...*letter to Monroe, June 17, 1785*

...its soul, its climate, its equality, liberty, laws, people, and manners. My God! how little do my countrymen know what precious blessings they are in possession of, and which no other people on earth enjoy!

...to keep the dreams alive...

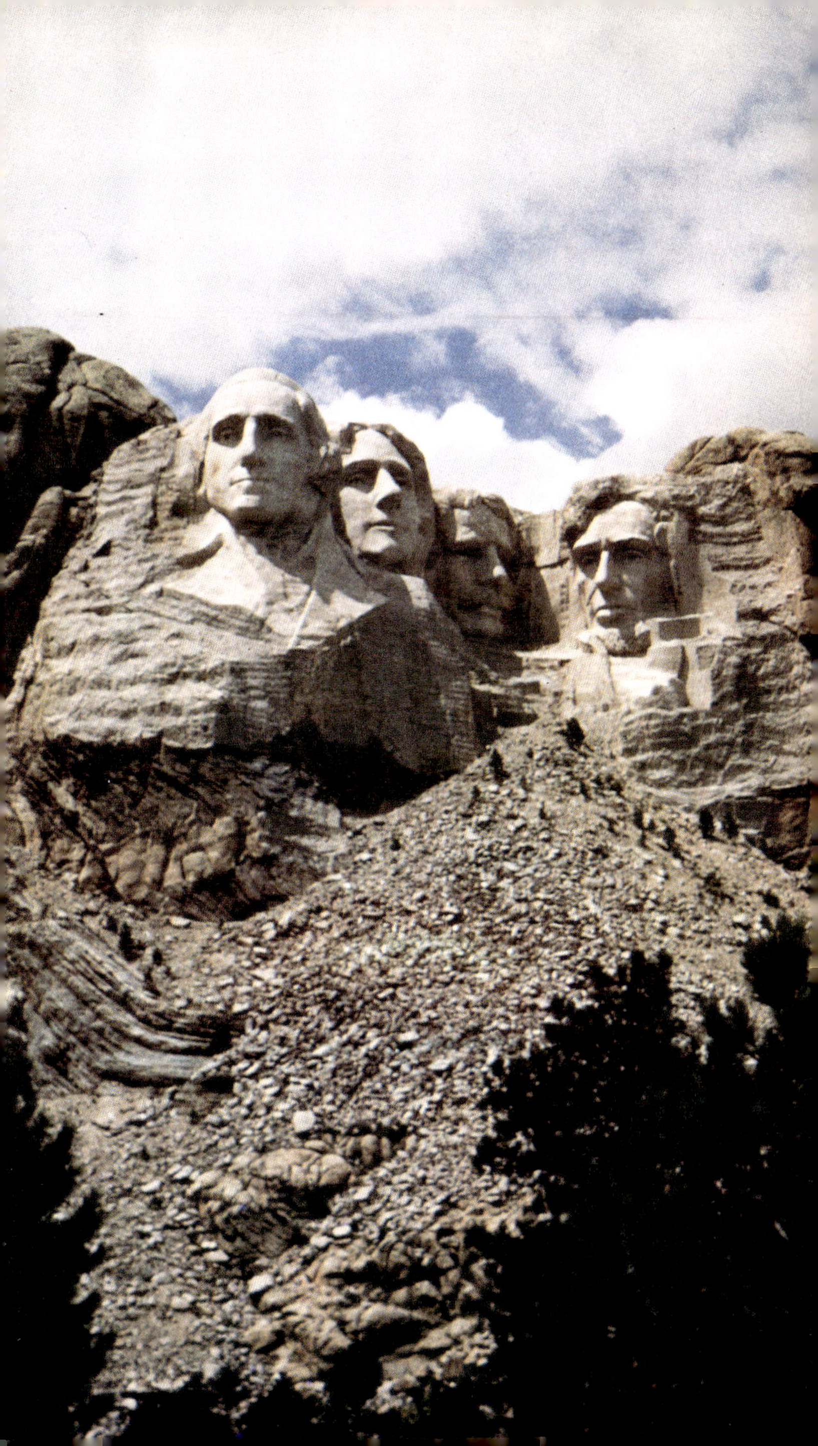

Robert Frost
The Gift Outright

The land was ours before we were the land's.
She was our land more than a hundred years
Before we were her people. She was ours
In Massachusetts, in Virginia,
But we were England's, still colonials,
Possessing what we still were unpossessed by,
Possessed by what we now no more possessed.
Something we were withholding made us weak
Until we found out that it was ourselves
We were withholding from our land of living,
And forthwith found salvation in surrender.
Such as we were we gave ourselves outright
(The deed of gift was many deeds of war)
To the land vaguely realizing westward,
But still unstoried, artless, unenhanced,
Such as she was, such as she would become.

Katharine Lee Bates
America the Beautiful

O beautiful for spacious skies,
For amber waves of grain,
For purple mountain majesties
Above the fruited plain!
America! America!
God shed His grace on thee
And crown thy good with brotherhood
From sea to shining sea!

O beautiful for pilgrim feet,
Whose stern, impassioned stress
A thoroughfare for freedom beat
Across the wilderness!
America! America!
God mend thine every flaw,
Confirm thy soul in self-control,
Thy liberty in law!

O beautiful for heroes proved
In liberating strife,
Who more than self their country loved,
And mercy more than life!
America! America!
May God thy gold refine
Till all success be nobleness
And every gain divine!

O beautiful for patriot dream
That sees beyond the years
Thine alabaster cities gleam
Undimmed by human tears!
America! America!
God shed His grace on thee
And crown thy good with brotherhood
From sea to shining sea!

Archibald MacLeish
...The Meaning of 'Moving West'

Because the movement of discoverers and conquerors and colonists was a movement from east to west across the Atlantic, and because the frontiersmen and the settlers moved across the continent from east to west, west has always been the direction of the future in American history. The American dream has been a dream of the west, of the world farther on. But now that the great journey across the ocean and the continent has come to...the coast of the Pacific, there are those who say we have come to the end of the dream also. We must look backward now, they say, not forward; we must fear, not hope; we must hate, not love; we must conform, not imagine. It is strange doctrine to hear from Americans. No man can come to the Pacific coast of this continent...and feel he has come to the *end* of anything.... California, it is quite true, has filled up with people: her valleys are richly farmed, her cities are among the greatest in the world, her industries are fabulous. But even so the American journey has not ended. America is never accomplished, America is always still to build; for men, as long as they are truly men, will dream of man's fulfillment. West is a country in the mind, and so eternal.

Lyman Abbott
...The American's Inheritance

A signed editorial article which appeared in The Outlook *in June, 1916.*

A nation is made great, not by its fruitful acres, but by the men who cultivate them; not by its great forests, but by the men who use them; not by its mines, but by the men who work in them; not by its railways, but by the men who build and run them. America was a great land when Columbus discovered it; Americans have made of it a great Nation....

Rose Kennedy
...A Land of Dedication and Dreams

From the Mayflower to Skylab, America was built with the hands of millions of ordinary citizens dedicated to making this country work. As one who has lived through several generations in the history of this nation, I have seen many different faces of America. I know that belief and commitment have been essential to all our past progress, and that they are the key to all our future hopes. Illusions may fade, but the dreams that have made this country great will never die, so long as there are men and women willing to work to keep the dreams alive and to hold the standard high.

Set in Goudy Old Style.
Printed on Crown Royale book paper.